The RightFight

Study Guide

The RightFight

Study Guide

JOHN KENNEDY VAUGHAN

BROWN
CHRISTIAN PRESS
A DIVISION OF
BROWN BOOKS PUBLISHING

The Right Fight Study Guide

Unless otherwise indicated, Scriptures are taken from the Holy Bible, New International Version®, NIV®. Copyright © 1973, 1978, 1984, 2011 by Biblica, Inc.™ Used by permission of Zondervan. All rights reserved worldwide, www.zondervan.com. The "NIV" and "New International Version" are trademarks registered in the United States Patent and Trademark Office by Biblica, Inc.™

Brown Christian Press
Dallas, TX/New York, NY
www.BrownChristianPress.com
(972) 381-0009

A New Era in Publishing®

Publisher's Cataloging-In-Publication Data

Names: Vaughan, John Kennedy, author. | Vaughan, John Kennedy. Right fight.
Title: The right fight study guide / John Kennedy Vaughan.
Description: Dallas, TX ; New York, NY : Brown Christian Press, a division of Brown Books Publishing, [2020] | Series: The right fight | A workbook to accompany The right fight.
Identifiers: ISBN 9781612543239
Subjects: LCSH: Love--Religious aspects--Christianity--Problems, exercises, etc. | God (Christianity)--Love--Problems, exercises, etc. | Fear--Religious aspects--Christianity--Problems, exercises, etc. | Choice (Psychology)--Religious aspects--Christianity--Problems, exercises, etc. | Christian life--Problems, exercises, etc. | LCGFT: Problems and exercises.
Classification: LCC BV4639 .V381 2020 | DDC 241.4--dc23

ISBN 978-1-61254-323-9
LCCN 2019940325

Printed in the United States
10 9 8 7 6 5 4 3 2 1

For more information or to contact the author,
please go to www.ShieldsofStrength.com.

Contents

How to Use This Book

Welcome to *The Right Fight Study Guide*! We're glad you've decided to pick up this study. It has been designed to help you engage thoughtfully and prayerfully with John Kennedy Vaughan's *The Right Fight: How to Live a Loving Life*, on your own or in a group. In both cases, we recommend using this book as a sixteen-week study, with an optional review at the end.

Before you complete each lesson, read its corresponding chapter in *The Right Fight*. Use the questions in this book to help you reflect on the ideas in each chapter and evaluate how you can, with the help of Christ, choose love over fear in every aspect of your life.

Using This Study on Your Own

This guide can be used for individual study, using the questions as journal prompts. Commit to studying a chapter a week. Pray as you consider each question. The application questions at the end of every lesson will be of special value in implementing the things you learn about love into your everyday life.

Working in a Group

While this study guide can be used by an individual, it may be also be used in an organized group setting, using the questions in each chapter to spark discussion. A group should commit to meeting once a week to discuss the questions in each chapter. Regular meetings and honest discussion can offer perspective, a support base, and accountability partners as the group members move forward in their journeys to discover love and become better soldiers in the fight against fears—in addition to the personal insight using this study may provide anyway.

Conclusion

We hope that you will find *The Right Fight Study Guide* useful in understanding and navigating the truths in *The Right Fight: How to Live a Loving Life*. Bible passages interspersed among the reflection questions are meant to direct attention to areas of further study in God's Word you may pursue independently. Visual organizers will help you brainstorm and lay out your thoughts on the page. Case studies in certain chapters illustrate the different choices people like you and me must make every day between love and fear. God bless you on your journey to live a loving life!

Ice Cream, My Kids, and My New Truck

Before We Begin

This study aims to walk you through ways you can choose love over fear and bear fruit in Christ in every aspect of your life. Each lesson, after reading the corresponding chapter of *The Right Fight: How to Live a Loving Life*, we will examine the concepts within and relevant passages of Scripture that speak to how you can reject fear and embrace love for others.

> Groups may want to take this time to discuss how they will set up this study. Will you meet weekly? Twice weekly? When?

As you participate in each lesson, be thinking about the different situations you face each day in your own life and the ways you choose to fear or love. Prayerfully consider how you can follow Jesus.

Going into Week One

1. What do you hope to get out of this study? List some goals you have for the next sixteen weeks.

   _____

   _____

_____

_____

_____

> Remember, you will get out what you put into this
> study! Make a commitment to reading along with *The
> Right Fight: How to Live a Loving Life* every week.

2.   How can you make the most of this study?

_____

_____

_____

_____

_____

Ice Cream and Trucks

We can choose to be loving every moment of every day of our lives. In this chapter, the author discusses a way in which he loved his family that he almost abandoned out of his fear for a prized possession. Opportunities to love or hurt others in your life may show up in mundane-seeming or unexpected ways. They can occur in quiet moments with your family and friends or in hectic ones, at work, at school, or on vacation.

Sharing a late-night ice cream run with family may not seem like a way to show love at first, but on reflection, you may find that many of the ways in which you've felt the love of others have been comparatively simple.

3. Define love.

_____

_____

_____

_____

_____

4. What does love mean to you?

_____

_____

_____

_____

5. Where do you see love in your everyday life?

_____

_____

_____

_____

While the author could show love to his children by taking them for spontaneous, late-night ice cream, he eventually found that, for him, taking away these trips to save the cleanliness of his new truck was a selfish act. Likewise, the choice to yell at his children for an accidental spill would come from his selfish fear for the truck rather than from his love for his children.

Like love, fear and selfishness can come in surprising forms in our day-to-day lives.

6. What does selfishness mean to you?

_____

_____

_____

_____

_____

7. Compare and contrast loving and unloving actions people take in their everyday lives. How might we not think about these at first?

Loving	Unloving

Sucking It Up

The author chose to "lovingly sacrifice" his own desires twice in this chapter for the sake of his children, first to reinstate the ice cream runs he enjoyed sharing with his family and second to forgive his daughter when her brother's acrobatics spilled ice cream on the unprotected dashboard of his truck.

Christians set an example not only to their children but also to unbelievers in their actions toward others. Sacrificing your own needs and desires to serve your neighbor can be a form of worship.

> Therefore, I urge you, brothers and sisters, in view of God's mercy, to offer your bodies as a living sacrifice, holy and pleasing to God—this is your true and proper worship.
>
> —Romans 12:1

8. In your opinion, what does it mean to "lovingly sacrifice yourself"?

_____

_____

_____

_____

_____

9. What does it *not* mean?

_____

_____

_____

_____

_____

10. The author states that people will forget what you say, but they will not forget how you make them feel. What do Christians' love or selfishness toward others tell them about our faith?

_____

_____

_____

_____

_____

APPLICATION

> Participants in a group may not wish to answer some of the more personal application questions aloud. Instead, think about these questions through the week. Feel free to use the workbook as a journal here. Start exploring how love and fear interact in your own life. Pray for God to open your heart to the people around you.

11. In this chapter, the author's fear for his truck temporarily held him back from being as loving toward his children as he wanted to be, but there are many other fears and desires that will hold us back from showing the love of Christ to others if we let them. Think of some of the attitudes that are holding you back from loving the people in your life.

_____

_____

_____

_____

_____

12. Who are some people in your life you can love more this week?

_____

_____

_____

_____

_____

13. What are some loving actions you can take this week?

_____

_____

_____

_____

_____

LESSON TWO

Strong Foundations

At the beginning of every week's lesson, take
some time to think about the previous week
and the ways you are applying its lessons
to your life. A group may wish to discuss
experiences they have had through the week.

REVIEW

Before you begin this week's study, take some time to reflect on last week's discussion on love and sacrifice.

1. Did you see love at work in new ways last week? Give some examples.

_____

_____

_____

_____

_____

2. Who have you loved this past week? In what ways?

_____

_____

_____

_____

_____

GOING BACK TO THE BASICS

In this chapter, the author writes about a time that he had to review and correct his fundamentals in order to improve in his sport. Although this experience was a humbling one, he found that returning to the basics of water skiing enabled him to correct his form and jump farther and better than ever before.

Like understanding proper form is essential to performing well at higher levels of water skiing, understanding love is essential to living a righteous and holy life. Jesus explains that every commandment God gives us stems from the same source: loving God and loving others.

> "'Love the Lord your God with all your heart and with all your soul and with all your mind.' This is the first and greatest commandment. And the second is like it: 'Love your neighbor as yourself.' All the Law and the Prophets hang on these two commandments."
>
> –Matthew 22:37–40

3. Have you ever been in a situation where, like the author, you have had to return to basic principles in order to advance toward a goal? Explain.

_____

_____

_____

_____

_____

4. How do fundamentals enable us to build a firm foundation for the future?

_____

_____

_____

_____

_____

5. Why do you think loving God and loving others is the root of all the commandments in the Bible?

_____

_____

_____

_____

_____

6. How does love serve as the fundamental principle for living a good life? Can you give an example of a time you realized you needed to be more loving in order to understand or communicate with others better?

_____

_____

_____

_____

_____

FEAR: THE ENEMY OF LOVE

The author achieved his dream of winning the national water ski tournament by returning to the fundamentals of the sport but also by casting out his fear of failure by dedicating his performance to the Lord and to the woman who later became his wife—banishing fear through his love for Jesus Christ and others.

Love is the foundation on which a healthy life is built, but fear can distract and paralyze us and keep us from living the life God wants for us.

7. What fears are distracting you from loving God and the people around you?

_____

_____

_____

_____

_____

8. In your workplace?

_____

_____

_____

_____

_____

9. In your ministry?

_____

_____

_____

_____

_____

10. At home and with your family?

_____

_____

_____

_____

_____

11. When the author took a catalog of his fears, he found that his fears were rooted in a focus on himself. Do you see a similar pattern in your own fears?

_____

_____

_____

_____

_____

> There is no fear in love. But perfect love drives out fear, because fear has to do with punishment. The one who fears is not made perfect in love.
>
> –1 John 4:18

12. If fear has to do with punishment—a hesitance to suffer pain, loss, or humiliation—how might love force fear out?

_____

_____

_____

_____

_____

APPLICATION

The most God wants from His people is that they be connected in relationship to Him and to one another. This single, basic fact is the beginning of a full and vibrant life in Christ. This week, spend

> Cast all your anxiety on him because he cares for you.
>
> –1 Peter 5:7

some time thinking about the fears you've identified in your life. How are they keeping you from the life God wants for you? How can love lay the foundation for your future?

13. What fears do you need to give to God this week? Pray to Him and let Him bear your burdens.

_____

_____

_____

_____

_____

14. If love is about looking outward to God and to others, who might you not have been seeing lately? How can you reach out to those around you this week?

_____

_____

_____

_____

_____

The Fruit and Roots of Love

REVIEW

Last week, we covered how love is the first and most important instruction of life—the foundation for all the rest—and how fear, an inward-looking focus on self, can keep us from connecting with others the way God intends us to.

1. How have you been more mindful of your fears this past week? Have you identified persistent obstacles in your journey to love God and others?

_____

_____

_____

_____

_____

2. What efforts have you made to refocus on God and others to love them better?

_____

_____

_____

_____

_____

FEELINGS ARE THE FRUIT OF LOVE; FEELINGS ARE NOT LOVE

Love is not a feeling. How controversial is that? All around, movies, music, and advertisements promote the idea that love is the passion you feel for a significant other or the warm, secure sense of being surrounded by family. Yet in 1 Corinthians 13, where the apostle Paul defines love, every part of it is a virtue that can be practiced—choices we as believers make to act in loving ways. Feelings come and go; love is forever.

> If I speak in the tongues of men or of angels, but do not have love, I am only a resounding gong or a clanging cymbal. If I have the gift of prophecy and can fathom all mysteries and all knowledge, and if I have a faith that can move mountains, but do not have love, I am nothing. If I give all I possess to the poor and give over my body to hardship that I may boast, but do not have love, I gain nothing.
>
> Love is patient, love is kind. It does not envy, it does not boast, it is not proud. It does not dishonor others, it is not self-seeking, it is not easily angered, it keeps no record of wrongs. Love does not delight in evil but rejoices with the truth. It always protects, always trusts, always hopes, always perseveres.
>
> Love never fails. But where there are prophecies, they will cease; where there are tongues, they will be stilled; where there is knowledge, it will pass away.
>
> –1 Corinthians 13:1–8

3. Do you believe love is a choice? Why or why not?

_____

_____

_____

_____

_____

4. In what ways is it freeing to view love as a choice we can make?

_____

_____

_____

_____

_____

Love is not a feeling, but when we are loved, we have feelings of friendliness, protectiveness, tenderness, closeness, or passion toward others. These feelings come from loving choices we make—choices to trust, hope, persevere, and put others before ourselves.

5. How do the loving choices others make inspire you to care for them?

_____

_____

_____

_____

_____

6. Are the choices you make inspiring others to care for you? In what ways?

_____

_____

_____

_____

_____

The feelings of value and belonging we get when we are loved are wonderful things, blessings God provides to emphasize the importance of loving Him and loving others. But when we allow these feelings to become our focus rather than the loving choices that lead to them, we are focusing inward once again, paying more attention to how we feel than what we are offering to others. The *fear* of losing these feelings begins to rule over us rather than our devotion to making the loving choices that has produced them.

7. How can a preoccupation on the feelings produced by love keep us from loving others?

_____

_____

_____

_____

_____

8. Consider the traits that define love in 1 Corinthians 13. How do you put them into practice in your everyday life?

What Love Is	Everyday Practice
Patient	
Kind	
Truthful	

What Love Is	Everyday Practice
Protective	
Trusting	
Hopeful	
Persistent	

9. From the same passage, consider the things that love is *not*. What kind of unloving choices do you make in your own life? How can you fight these tendencies to live a more loving life?

What Love Is Not	How I Can Fight This Tendency
Angry	
Rude	
Envious	
Prideful	
Unforgiving	

What Love Is Not	How I Can Fight This Tendency
Boastful	
Selfish	
Malicious	

On our own, we cannot grow the fruit of love. In order to have healthy, fruit-producing roots, we need to be *rooted in* something—namely, in Jesus Christ. A relationship with God provides us with the strength to produce the fruit that blesses us and others.

10. Are your roots connected to Christ? How can you take your strength from Him?

_____

_____

_____

_____

_____

When we don't trust our lives to Christ—when we try to take control back because we have been hurt or are afraid of loss—we don't receive the nourishment we need to be fruitful, productive, and loving. Though it can be painful to be taken advantage of and to have blessings stripped away from us—to have fruit taken from our trees—continuing to abide in love will always restore us. Choosing instead to react to the pain with anger, distrust, and retaliation cuts off our roots from Christ.

> Dear friends, let us love one another, for love comes from God. Everyone who loves has been born of God and knows God. Whoever does not love does not know God, because God is love.
>
> –1 John 4:7–8

11. What kinds of hurt tempt you most to try and take control back from God? In what fearful ways are you most likely to react?

_____

_____

_____

_____

_____

12. What does it mean to you to know that God's love produces the fruit of love in your life?

_____

_____

_____

_____

_____

"I am the vine; you are the branches. If you remain in me and I in you, you will bear much fruit; apart from me you can do nothing. If you do not remain in me, you are like a branch that is thrown away and withers; such branches are picked up, thrown into the fire and burned. If you remain in me and my words remain in you, ask whatever you wish, and it will be done for you. This is to my Father's glory, that you bear much fruit, showing yourselves to be my disciples.

"As the Father has loved me, so have I loved you. Now remain in my love. If you keep my commands, you will remain in my love, just as I have kept my Father's commands and remain in his love."

–John 15:5–10

13. What purpose do the blessings or fruit God gives you serve?

_____

_____

_____

_____

_____

FENCES OF FEAR

Sometimes, we can have every intention of acting with love toward others, but our reluctance to allow ourselves to be hurt can lead us to establish boundaries that keep others at a safe distance. We believe this is the smart thing to do. *Stupid to invite people to hurt you, right?* we think. *Boundaries are smart. Healthy, even.* Yet when we try to take control of our lives by pushing others out to arm's length, we are acting out of fear and trusting ourselves—and our boundaries—instead of God.

As the author notes in chapter 3, however, there is a difference between holding people at arm's length to save ourselves from pain and refusing to allow them to make unloving choices that will hurt them in the long run. Remember: love is about doing what is best for others, always.

14. Give an example of a time when you have drawn a boundary between yourself and others in an attempt to save yourself from pain.

_____

_____

_____

_____

_____

15. When have you done the opposite? Done what is best for others regardless of the benefit or consequence to yourself?

_____

_____

_____

_____

_____

Love's Defense

While building walls is a fearful solution to experiencing hurt, encouraging those who hurt us to act in love instead offers them the best opportunity to change. Acting in love is its own shield. In this chapter, the author discusses how the truth serves as a defense for those who act in love.

16. How does truth serve as a witness and defender when others hurt you?

_____

_____

_____

_____

_____

17. Why do we tell the truth if we are acting in love?

_____

_____

_____

_____

_____

> "But I tell you, do not resist an evil person.
> If anyone slaps you on the right cheek,
> turn to them the other cheek also."
>
> –Matthew 5:39

18. What is the benefit of refusing to shield ourselves when we come under attack? Why do you think Jesus instructed us not to resist when others try to harm us?

_____

_____

_____

_____

_____

FORGIVING OTHERS IN LOVE

19. In order to continue abiding in love, we need to forgive others when they wrong us. How does our forgiveness or lack thereof prove our love for others?

_____

_____

_____

_____

_____

In chapter 3, the author explains that when others harm us, they break God's law of love and become a debtor against us. In the same sense that a criminal must pay a debt to society when they break one of society's laws, a sinner owes a debt to the person they sin against and to God. Yet if we retaliate against them and enforce payment, we break God's law of love ourselves. Forgiveness means instead absorbing the cost of the debt ourselves—the same way Jesus absorbed the cost of our sins on the cross.

20. It's not wrong to feel the need for justice when others hurt you. David often wrote psalms asking God for justice against his enemies. How can you give your pain to God?

_____

_____

_____

_____

_____

21. Why should you make the effort to forgive others despite the cost?

_____

_____

_____

_____

_____

APPLICATION

We all want the fruit that is the blessings of love in our lives, but if we are to enjoy it and continue producing it, we must remain focused on its source: the love of God and the actions we take out of that love every day. This week, take some time to consider how you can better connect to the roots of all love in your life.

> Then Peter came to Jesus and asked, "Lord, how many times shall I forgive my brother or sister who sins against me? Up to seven times?" Jesus answered, "I tell you, not seven times, but seventy-seven times."
>
> – Matthew 18:21–22

22. Everyone struggles in some way with giving God control. In what ways do you need to abide more in God's love and let his commandments and grace rule your life?

_____

_____

_____

_____

_____

23. What fear-related boundaries might you need to tear down?

_____

_____

_____

_____

_____

24. Who might you need to forgive?

_____

_____

_____

_____

_____

Living Inside Out

REVIEW

Last week, we studied how maintaining healthy roots of patience, kindness, truthfulness, protectiveness, trust, hope, and perseverance by drawing our nourishment from a relationship with God can drive out fears and produce the fruit of love in our lives.

1. Explain how fear can wither the roots of love in our lives. Can you give an example?

_____

_____

_____

_____

_____

2. What actions should we avoid in order to keep our roots connected and healthy?

_____

_____

_____

_____

_____

3. What actions should we take?

_____

_____

_____

_____

_____

CHOOSING LOVE OVER FEAR

In chapter 4 of *The Right Fight*, the author discusses how we must examine our actions—and those of the people around us—to choose love instead of fear every day.

4. The author lists family interactions, parenting decisions, business, and athletic endeavors as some of the areas where we might need to examine our actions to choose love over fear. Brainstorm some areas in which you might be called on to choose love over fear.

Where and How Do I Need to Love?

Love (n.):

A profoundly tender, passionate
affection for another person.
A feeling of warm, personal attachment or deep
affection, as for a parent, child, or friend.
Sexual passion or desire.
A person toward whom love is felt.
Beloved person; sweetheart.

5. Above are the dictionary definitions of love. Compare them to the personal definition you gave in lesson 1 of this study. How has your personal definition changed since then?

_____

_____

_____

_____

_____

6. What do you think is missing from the popular conception of love? What is a better definition of love?

_____

_____

_____

_____

_____

LOVE SEEKS THE HIDDEN TRUTHS

As the author points out in chapter 4, if we aren't careful, we can judge others by their actions while expecting them to respond to our intentions. It's important to consider the hidden motivations behind the choices of others in our dealings with them, just as we expect others to have compassion for our good intentions when they are dealing with

Use the case studies in this book to consider how the principles you are studying play out in real life. Respond to them in a journal or discuss them in a group setting. Try and imagine how similar situations might arise in your own life.

us. When we consider the hidden difficulties others may be experiencing, we will be compassionate and merciful toward them. If we respond only to the surface failures we perceive, we may choose to become angry instead, cutting off the roots of love in our life.

7. The author relates a time when he was tempted to respond in anger when a seemingly careless waitress neglected him at a special dinner he only gets to enjoy once a year. Describe a time you wanted to respond in anger or actually did so. What was the result?

_____

_____

_____

_____

_____

Consider the following two case studies. Think about the fear and irritation you might experience in such a situation. How might you want to respond? What would be the more loving decision? What hidden truths might lie beneath the surface? How would knowing them change your behavior?

Seeking Hidden Truths: Case Study #1

A teacher often deals with apathetic or unmotivated students, but in Riley Owens, Ms. Smith had thought she saw a rare and welcome exception. Riley always turned in assignments on time, complete. Riley was attentive and engaged in class, and Riley's answers showed thoughtfulness and encouraged other students to engage with the material.

After midterms, however, Riley's engagement began to drop off. Riley had already scored high enough on enough assignments that Riley was nearly guaranteed an A in the class. Ms. Smith had seen students frontload their work in her class before, doing enough work to receive the grade they wanted so they could blow off the rest of the class, but she had believed Riley was sincerely interested in learning.

The night before a major assignment was due, Ms. Smith went out to supper with her family. As she left the restaurant, she saw Riley talking earnestly with two other students in another booth. None of the students noticed her, and she didn't want to interrupt.

The next morning, when the assignment was due, Riley came up to Ms. Smith after class and asked for an extension on the project.

1. What fears might Ms. Smith have in this situation?
2. How might she want to respond?
3. Love requires us to seek the truth in every situation. Love also requires us not to allow others to harm themselves. How should Ms. Smith seek the truth of Riley's situation?
4. What is the loving response if she discovers there is more to Riley's recent lack of effort in her class than there appears to be?
5. What is the loving response if she discovers Riley has indeed lost focus in her class because Riley is all but guaranteed an A?

Seeking Hidden Truths: Case Study #2

Andy Cohen is a devoted son. Every week he has lunch with his father, Fred, after church on Sunday, and he tries to visit his father's home on another occasion at least once a month. Since the death of Andy's mother, Giana, last year, Fred's health has been declining. Andy's responsibilities to his workplace and his other family members mean he cannot attend to his father's health needs as often as he would like to, so he has hired a nurse to look in on his father twice a week.

Recently, visits with Fred have become much more difficult. Fred has become extremely critical of Andy and the rest of Andy's family. He is negative about the news, about his neighbors, and about the people passing in the streets. He is forgetful and dismissive of the events that matter to Andy, Andy's wife, Karen, and to their children. Fred's nurse, Rory, reports that Fred does not follow instructions, loses his temper easily, and is occasionally verbally abusive during their check-ups as well.

Andy doesn't know what to do. He loves his father, but Fred is making it difficult to care for him, and Andy is reluctant to expose Karen and the rest of their family to his father's increasing negativity.

1. What fears might Andy have in this situation?

2. How might he want to respond?

3. Love requires us to seek the truth in every situation. Love also requires us to be protective of everyone in our lives. How should Andy seek the truth of Fred's situation?

4. What are some ways in which Andy can choose to love his father if he discovers there is more to Fred's increasing anger and negativity than meets the eye?

5. What are some ways in which Andy can choose to love the rest of his family if Fred continues to choose anger?

8. Through the intervention of his children, the author was able to respond with grace when he felt neglected, and he discovered that there had been severely extenuating circumstances recently in his waitress's life. Describe a time when you looked for hidden truths before responding in anger. What was the result?

_____

_____

_____

_____

_____

9. Though seeking the hidden motivations behind people's actions can help us have compassion for them in a way we might not otherwise have done, sometimes we discover that their actions are still motivated by fear. When others hurt us out of a place of fear, why is continuing to respond in love a better choice in the long term?

_____

_____

_____

_____

_____

10. If we instead act upon our feelings of hurt and choose anger, rudeness, or pride, what is the long-term impact of this decision?

_____

_____

_____

_____

_____

APPLICATION

We all define ourselves every day by the loving and fearful decisions we make. Considering the actions of others from the inside out can help us act with love toward them, ensuring that their fearful actions do not spark a fearful or angry response from us and cut us off from the roots of love. This week, practice living from the inside out.

11. Think of someone whose actions you have judged in the past. What are some ways you can get to know them better and seek the truth motivating their actions?

_____

_____

_____

_____

_____

12. What ways do you think living from the inside out can impact your decisions this week?

_____

_____

_____

_____

_____

13. What actions can you take this week to live a loving life from the inside out?

_____

_____

_____

_____

_____

Choosing Fear

REVIEW

Chapter 4 of *The Right Fight* deals with how, instead of hypocritically asking others to judge us according to our intentions while we judge others by their actions, we should search for the hidden truths behind the actions of others in an effort to show compassion.

1. Explain what it means to live inside out. How is this different from our first instincts?

_____

_____

_____

_____

_____

2. Why is it important for us to act with love and compassion toward others, regardless of the ways in which they act toward us?

_____

_____

_____

_____

_____

FEARFUL CHOICES

Like the dictionary definition of love outlines instead some popular misconceptions of what love is, the dictionary definition of fear fails to explain the terrible outcomes of making choices out of fear. The author notes in chapter 5 of *The Right Fight* that "love is an action or a choice that results in a feeling, whereas fear is a feeling that can result in an action." For this reason, it can be difficult to act out of love instead of fear; our instinct as human beings is to act on the emotions we have instead of reason or principles beyond them. A better understanding of the feelings born of fear in our lives can help us avoid making choices out of that fear.

> Fear (n.):
>
> A distressing emotion aroused by impending danger, evil, or pain, whether the threat is real or imagined. The feeling or condition of being afraid.

3. Have you ever been told to "follow your heart" or "trust your gut"? Why is this the wrong advice? What traps can living based on your emotions lead you into?

_____

_____

_____

_____

_____

> The heart is deceitful above all things and
> beyond cure. Who can understand it?
>
> –Jeremiah 17:9

4. How can realizing you are in control of your own actions help you calm the emotions stirred up by the actions of others that you can't control?

_____

_____

_____

_____

_____

A More Complete Definition of Fear

The blessings of love are brought about by the loving choices a person makes, and the barrenness of a person who is living in fear is likewise brought about by their choices. Someone who feels a moment of anger or envy or has a selfish thought is not a fearful person until they act out of their feelings. But when we choose to let these feelings control us, they define us until we make another choice to change.

5. Describe the difference between feeling and acting on feelings of anger. How can we control our actions so we do not let our anger define us?

_____

_____

_____

_____

_____

6. Times we feel the desire to be rude may be the best times to seek the hidden truths behind the feelings and actions of others. We can start to show patience and compassion instead. What are some ways we can slow our hastiness to judge and take time to understand in the heat of the moment?

_____

_____

_____

_____

_____

7. Envy is rooted in the fears of *not having enough* and of *being overshadowed or forgotten*. In a fallen world filled with want, injustice, and inequality,

everyone experiences feelings of envy from time to time. How should we respond in moments we feel envy? How can we keep our moments of envy from defining us?

_____

_____

_____

_____

_____

8. The author characterizes pride as a feeling more serious than others listed in chapter 5. While envious, rude, or angry feelings, for example, may merely be responses to difficult or frustrating circumstances in our lives, pride is an indication that our sense of reality has become warped. What are the two antidotes the author names for pride?

_____

_____

_____

_____

_____

9. Explain how we harm ourselves when we refuse to forgive others. Can you give an example?

_____

_____

_____

_____

_____

10. While pride is the result of a warped view of ourselves and our place in the world, boasting is our attempt to warp others' perceptions of us and our place in the world out of fear we may otherwise be seen as weak. How is the truth stronger than a boast?

_____

_____

_____

_____

_____

11. The author claims "we are always becoming either more or less selfish, depending on how much we choose to love." How do selfish or loving actions train us to be selfish or loving individuals?

_____

_____

_____

_____

_____

12. Like pride, delighting in evil is a sign that there is already something wrong in the way we see the world—and delighting in evil is the worse one. Name the ways the author describes that a person may delight in evil.

_____

_____

_____

_____

_____

APPLICATION

This week, take some time to think about the fearful feelings you experience on a day-to-day basis and the fearful behaviors that may have popped up in your life. These are the fights you will have to win in order to stay rooted in love.

13. What is one fearful behavior you can work on changing this week? Remember, fearful feelings do not have to control you.

_____

_____

_____

_____

_____

14. What are some strategies you can use to keep from being controlled by your fearful feelings?

_____

_____

_____

_____

_____

LESSON SIX

What Is Love?

REVIEW

Last week, we took a closer look at the different emotions and behaviors that can result from fear. Remember, feeling fear does not mean we have to act on it, cutting off our roots from love.

1. What is the difference between pride, delighting in evil, and feelings like anger, resentment, or envy? Explain.

_____

_____

_____

_____

_____

2. What are some of the ways choosing fear can harm us?

_____

_____

_____

_____

_____

For a group: Discuss how reading God's Word, prayer, and meditation can keep us rooted in Him and acting on His instincts instead of our own fallen ones. Also discuss other actions we can take to practice calmness and patience instead of anger and selflessness instead of selfishness. Some examples:

- Volunteering as a way to actively work for the good of others instead of ourselves.
- Scripture memorization to fall back on in times of high stress.
- Breathing routines.
- Open communication to help us process our emotions instead of bottling them up or dwelling on them.

3. What are some of the ways we can control our fearful instincts?

_____

_____

_____

_____

_____

Choosing Love Instead

If we choose to believe the popular definition of love, we will believe that love is something that happens to us, something outside of our control. If we instead believe the definition the apostle Paul provides in 1 Corinthians 13, we will come to realize that loving others is a choice we can make regardless of how we feel.

4. The author defines love in chapter 6 as "an undefeatable benevolence, an uncon-
    querable goodwill that always seeks the highest good of others, no matter what
    they do." How would believing this definition of love change your thoughts and
    actions on a day-to-day basis?

    _____

    _____

    _____

    _____

    _____

The tender feelings we have toward others—spouses, parents, siblings, and
friends—are commonly thought to be love but are in fact its result. But fighting just to
feel this way is *not* the *right fight*. Only when we put our focus on loving others—the
choices we make toward them in line with a higher principle or calling—will love
instead of fear rule our lives.

5. How does choosing the seven things love is produce the fruit of love in our lives?
    Why is it important to focus on making loving choices instead of how we feel
    because of them?

    _____

    _____

    _____

    _____

    _____

LOVING CHOICES

6. One thing that's important to remember is that love grows best in situations where it might be easier to be unloving. This is perhaps most obvious on a day-to-day basis with patience. Name some common situations where you're called on to practice patience.

_____

_____

_____

_____

_____

If I speak in the tongues of men or of angels, but do not have love, I am only a resounding gong or a clanging cymbal. If I have the gift of prophecy and can fathom all mysteries and all knowledge, and if I have a faith that can move mountains, but do not have love, I am nothing. If I give all I possess to the poor and give over my body to hardship that I may boast, but do not have love, I gain nothing.

Love is patient, love is kind. It does not envy, it does not boast, it is not proud. It does not dishonor others, it is not self-seeking, it is not easily angered, it keeps no record of wrongs. Love does not delight in evil but rejoices with the truth. It always protects, always trusts, always hopes, always perseveres.

Love never fails. But where there are prophecies, they will cease; where there are tongues, they will be stilled; where there is knowledge, it will pass away.

–1 Corinthians 13:1–8

7. "Letting others have their way all the time—indulgence—is often mistaken for kindness and love. In reality, it is selfishness and fear. Kind is always nice—in the long run—but niceness in the short run may not always be kind."

Use this space to list some examples of some situations where kindness might mean allowing others to be uncomfortable or even experience pain.

When It's Kinder Not to Be Nice

8. In lesson 4, we discussed how it's important to search for hidden truths in the experiences and intentions of others so can act with wisdom and compassion toward them, but love can go farther than that in seeking truth. How can truth illuminate our own actions and help us be more loving?

---

9. We often try to "protect" friends and family from truths we feel could hurt them by telling "white lies" or shielding them from reality. Why is this not the loving thing to do? How can telling the truth even in the most difficult situations provide better protection?

    _____

    _____

    _____

    _____

    _____

10. While we should always tell others the truth, the truths we tell should always build others up. How can you protect others with your words?

    _____

    _____

    _____

    _____

    _____

11. The author distinguishes between choosing to trust someone toward whom you may not feel trusting and continuing to trust someone who has repeatedly abused your trust and shows no desire to change. Why is it sometimes loving to forgive and trust others again and sometimes loving to walk away? Explain.

    _____

    _____

    _____

    _____

    _____

> Now faith is confidence in what we hope for
> and assurance about what we do not see.
>
> –Hebrews 11:1

12. Why is it important you continue to hope in God and in others?

_____

_____

_____

_____

_____

13. How can trust, hope, and perseverance work together to ensure love never fails?

_____

_____

_____

_____

_____

> For in this hope we were saved. But hope that
> is seen is no hope at all. Who hopes for what
> they already have? But if we hope for what
> we do not yet have, we wait for it patiently.
>
> –Romans 8:24–25

APPLICATION

Remember, one fearful decision can define you in a moment but does not have to define you forever. Every day and every hour, you can decide to live a life ruled by love. This week, think about some areas in your life in which you can show more love.

14. In which situations is it hardest for you to show love? Do you find it hardest to be patient? To be kind? To trust or to protect others? Your answers might illuminate some fears you are still struggling with.

_____

_____

_____

_____

_____

15. Who are some people in your life you can love more this week?

_____

_____

_____

_____

_____

16. What are some loving actions you can take this week?

_____

_____

_____

_____

_____

Feelings Don't Produce Roots

REVIEW

In lesson 6, we discussed the loving choices we can make to stay rooted in love and produce blessings in our lives and our relationships. Lesson 7 discusses in more detail how these choices are not dependent on the emotions we may or may not feel. Before you begin studying more about the circumstances in which we make—and do not make—loving choices, take some time to recall what real love looks like in life.

1. What is the result of love? What causes love to grow? How are these two things often confused?

    _____

    _____

    _____

    _____

    _____

2. Why is it important to focus on living a loving life instead of on the blessings love produces in your life?

    _____

    _____

_____

_____

_____

You Don't Need to Feel Loving to Show Love

Chapter 7 discusses how if we allow our emotions to determine the choices we make and how we treat others, our emotions may mislead us. We may decide to *react* in fear instead of *acting* in love. Remember, we may feel angry or envious in response to various circumstances in our lives, but it is only when we choose to act on these feelings that our lives are ruled by fear.

Sometimes we will not feel loving toward others. We will feel tired or overwhelmed or anxious instead, but when we choose to persist in patience, kindness, truth, forgiveness, hope, trust, and protectiveness toward others, we will grow stronger in love for making those decisions when we didn't feel like it, and love will truly rule our lives.

3. How does reacting to situations according to your feelings give others the control? How does acting on truth and principle instead help you keep it?

_____

_____

_____

_____

_____

Tending Your Roots

Love is the best of good habits. Like proper nutrition and exercise, good financial practices, or dressing well and practicing good hygiene, once we begin to see the results of living loving lives—in the courage and peace that grows in our own lives and in the way we begin to bless others—it becomes more difficult to make selfish, fearful choices.

Think about the difference between acting and reacting. In effect, this is the difference between choosing your own course and being driven by your emotions. A person who takes personal responsibility for their own choices, regardless of what they might feel, will always be more in command of themselves and their lives than someone who spends their time reacting to fearful impulses.

4. Discuss a time when you were afraid of being selfish or of hurting someone else. Why did you feel that way?

_____

_____

_____

_____

_____

Remember that there is a difference between fearing a loss of someone's good opinion or their affection for you (a loss of the fruit or blessings they provide in your life) and fearing making a selfish choice and what that will do to you and your relationship long term (cutting off the roots that sustain you both).

5. Remember the lesson of John 15:5. What does it mean to abide in Christ? Can you do that regardless of your feelings?

_____

_____

_____

_____

_____

Love and Feelings: Case Study #1

Casey Rodriguez is a productive member of the team in the workplace. Not only is Casey willing to work long hours on projects with a hard deadline, Casey has also been quick to offer assistance to coworkers.

Last week, a client was dissatisfied with the service she was provided. Casey and a coworker, Shawn, were involved in the disagreement, and when Casey's boss, Mr. Weekes, was called to resolve the disagreement, Shawn told him that Casey's handling of the situation had resulted in the loss of the client, even though Casey had adhered to company policy through the situation. Casey received a reprimand, and the situation blew over, but Casey still feels hurt and betrayed by Shawn's unjust accusations—as well as by the fact that Mr. Weekes believed them.

This week, Casey has been assigned to work on a project with Shawn. Casey does not feel that Shawn can be trusted and feels resentful of Shawn sharing in the credit if the project goes well. Nevertheless, Casey can decide how to treat Shawn for the duration of the project.

1. How might Casey's feelings tempt them to a fearful reaction in this situation?

2. What could happen if Casey chooses to be led by feelings of distrust and resentment while working on the project with Shawn?

3. What choices could Casey make in order to allow love to continue to rule their life, despite their feelings?

4. What could be some long-term benefits of Casey choosing to treat Shawn with love and kindness, even after Shawn's betrayal?

6. The fruit of living a loving life takes the form of blessings we both receive and give to others. These can take the form of material possessions, but the blessings of a loving life are not only material possessions, and someone with very few material possessions at all can be living a blessed life. What does the fruit of a loving life actually look like?

_____

_____

_____

_____

_____

7. In contrast, what does a fruitless, fearful life look like? Explain.

_____

_____

_____

_____

_____

8. What does it mean to take personal responsibility for our choices? How does someone choose love over fear, regardless of their personal feelings?

_____

_____

_____

_____

_____

Love and Feelings: Case Study #2

On three separate occasions, Sam Stewart's sister Alison has taken money from Sam's wallet without asking. The amounts were small—twenty or forty dollars each time—and if Alison had asked, Sam would not have refused to give her the money. But the intrusion into Sam's privacy and the theft still feels invasive. In addition, over the last few months, Alison has, several times, canceled scheduled plans with Sam at the last minute, offering a vague excuse or none at all.

Sam is growing concerned about Alison. At their family dinner last week, Sam took Alison aside to express this concern, and Alison reacted with anger. She dismissed her thefts, claiming asking wasted time since Sam would have given her the money anyway, and deflected blame for the missed plans back on Sam for neglecting to consider Alison's exhaustion and her busy schedule.

Sam feels Alison is being unfair, thoughtless, and selfish. Alison's angry outburst has left Sam feeling angry as well, but Sam gets to decide how to respond to Alison now.

1. How might Sam's feelings of hurt, confusion, and anger tempt them to a reaction rooted in fear in this situation?

2. Love requires us to seek the truth in every situation. Can you imagine some truths Sam might miss about Alison if Sam chooses to let fear lead instead?

3. What kind of response could Sam make to Alison that would allow love to continue to rule their life, despite their feelings?

4. What could be some long-term benefits of Sam choosing to be patient and forgiving toward Alison, even after Alison's confusing behavior and angry outburst?

Your Feelings When Others Hurt You

Like Casey and Sam in the case studies presented in this chapter, as we go through life, others will take advantage of us and betray us, sometimes those we trust and love most of all. Their actions are outside of our control. What we feel because of those actions may be outside of our control—but how we respond to them is absolutely, 100 percent up to us. We can choose to be ruled by love, or we can give in to our fear.

When others consciously choose to hurt, betray, or take advantage of us (as opposed to times when we may simply misunderstand one another), they are the ones who are letting fear and selfishness rule over their lives. When we respond to hurtful actions in love, the blessings or fruit they have stolen will eventually return.

9. How do people hurt themselves when they choose to trespass on the rights of others or take advantage of the blessings in others' lives?

_____

_____

_____

_____

_____

10. How do we maintain the fruit in our lives when others can take it whenever they choose?

_____

_____

_____

_____

APPLICATION

Living a life ruled by love is a matter of choosing to do so. This week, consider how you can take control back, refuse to be led by your emotions, and respond to others in love no matter what.

11. Who are some people you have had difficulty responding to in love in the past? How can you work to avoid letting emotions control you when you encounter these people in the future?

_____

_____

_____

_____

_____

12. What are some loving actions you can take this week?

_____

_____

_____

_____

_____

Religion or Love?

REVIEW

You have studied the eight things fear is and the seven things love is and discussed that while everyone may have fearful feelings from time to time, it is the choices we make and not our feelings that determine whether fear or love rules our lives. Take a moment to review the differences between feelings and love.

1. Who or what is in control when we choose to respond to immediate feelings? Why is this a bad idea?

   _____

   _____

   _____

   _____

   _____

2. What happens when we choose to act in a loving manner regardless of our feelings?

   _____

   _____

   _____

_____

_____

CHRISTIANITY: A RELATIONSHIP, NOT A RELIGION

Despite our best efforts, on our own power we will all eventually fail to live lives led by love. Romans 3:23 states that "all have sinned and fall short of the glory of God"—the perfect love we are all called upon to exhibit toward God and others all the time. Some of you reading *The Right Fight* and working through this study guide might be offended by that. You may feel urged toward religion, but actually, Christianity is *not* meant to be a *religion* but a *relationship*.

In common usage, religion means the practice of certain rituals and observances in order to receive a desired outcome—giving to receive something. If you are a good person and faithful to certain tenets, you will be either protected from evil or granted blessings. Abiding in Christ, the soil we all need to maintain healthy roots of love, is different from this in that, in truth, God could not care less about the practice of any ritual observance. He is always interested first and most in the state of our hearts and in friendship and communion with His beloved creation. There are numerous places in the Old and New Testament that show us this. Consider a few of them below:

> But the Lord said to Samuel, "Do not consider his appearance or his height, for I have rejected him. The Lord does not look at the things people look at. People look at the outward appearance, but the Lord looks at the heart."
>
> –1 Samuel 16:17

> For You do not delight in sacrifice, or I would bring it; You take no pleasure in burnt offerings. The sacrifices of God are a broken spirit; a broken and a contrite heart, O God, You will not despise.
>
> –Psalm 51:16–17

> I hate, I despise your feasts! I cannot stand
> the stench of your solemn assemblies.
> Even though you offer Me burnt offerings
> and grain offerings, I will not accept
> them; for your peace offerings of fattened
> cattle, I will have no regard. Take away
> from Me the noise of your songs! I will
> not listen to the music of your harps.
> But let justice roll on like a river, and
> righteousness like an ever-flowing stream.
>
> –Amos 5:21-24

One of the best passages in the Bible on the way God's love in us comes from a place of relationship and not religious ritual is in 1 John 4. John explains how the salvation Christ grants His followers is a free gift, given out of love, and every part of living like a Christian is not to obtain that salvation but an act of gratitude and relationship, a free gift we give God in return because we love Him and because *we have already been saved.*

> Dear friends, let us love one another, for love comes
> from God. Everyone who loves has been born of God
> and knows God. Whoever does not love does not know
> God, because God is love. This is how God showed his
> love among us: He sent his one and only Son into the
> world that we might live through him. This is love: not
> that we loved God, but that he loved us and sent his Son

as an atoning sacrifice for our sins. Dear friends, since God so loved us, we also ought to love one another. No one has ever seen God; but if we love one another, God lives in us and his love is made complete in us.

This is how we know that we live in him and he in us: He has given us of his Spirit. And we have seen and testify that the Father has sent his Son to be the Savior of the world. If anyone acknowledges that Jesus is the Son of God, God lives in them and they in God. And so we know and rely on the love God has for us.

God is love. Whoever lives in love lives in God, and God in them. This is how love is made complete among us so that we will have confidence on the day of judgment: In this world we are like Jesus. There is no fear in love. But perfect love drives out fear, because fear has to do with punishment. The one who fears is not made perfect in love.

We love because he first loved us.

—1 John 4:7–19

In contrast, other faiths practiced around the world are religions. Salvation and blessing depend upon a person's actions. Consider some of the other commonly practiced religions around the world.

A Look at Some Major World Religions	
Islam[1]	• Followers of Islam believe they serve the same one god, called Allah. • Believe Jesus was a prophet, born of a virgin, but not the Son of God. • Believe in a Day of Judgement where followers of Islam will be rewarded with a place in heaven and unbelievers will be sentenced to Hell. • Following Islam requires adherence to the five pillars of faith—a profession of faith, five prayers daily, giving alms to the poor, fasting at certain times each year, and making a pilgrimage to Mecca once in a lifetime—but also observance of certain rules of diet, dress, and behavior.
Hinduism	• Followers of Hindu spirituality may believe in one god or many.[2] • The goal of Hinduism is to attain "dharma"—worldly contentment and happiness in this life and in any reincarnations, and to spare ourselves suffering through the practice of virtue and maintaining purity.[3] • Hindus may observe many rituals in order to bring themselves closer to the gods and become more meritorious individuals worthy of blessing.

A Look at Some Major World Religions

Buddhism	• For Buddhists, belief in God or gods is beside the point and maybe even detrimental. • Buddhists seek, through experience, to help themselves achieve enlightenment—detachment from greed, and thus, freedom from the suffering that ensues when desires are unmet.[4] • Enlightenment is achieved by following the Eightfold Path, a system of discipline, concentration, ethical and nonharmful conduct in everyday life, and dedication to unselfishness and righteous intent.[5]
Judaism	• Followers of Judaism believe in the God of the Old Testament of the Bible. Their primary holy text is the first five books—Genesis, Exodus, Leviticus, Numbers, and Deuteronomy. • Followers of Judaism believe that Jesus was just a man and a false Messiah.[6] • Jewish people seek the favor of God on Earth and harmony with the community of faith through adherence to 613 laws in the Torah. Sin—transgression against these commandments—can be forgiven, but forgiveness does not necessarily mean sin does not have consequences both earthly and divine.[7] Those who follow God's commandments receive His blessing, those who break them will be punished.

Islam, Hinduism, Buddhism, and Judaism, alongside Christianity, are the most widely practiced faiths on earth, but as you can see, even Buddhism—which ostensibly focuses on unselfish detachment from greed—has an end goal, namely the elimination of suffering. In every *religion*, people who believe are meant to follow certain practices in order to achieve a goal. In Christianity, Christ has already achieved the goal for us. The focus shifts to the love of God, our love for Him, and the relationship between us.

3. How is a relationship different than a bargain? Explain.

_____

_____

_____

_____

_____

One of the criminals who hung there hurled insults at him: "Aren't you the Messiah? Save yourself and us!"

But the other criminal rebuked him. "Don't you fear God," he said, "since you are under the same sentence? We are punished justly, for we are getting what our deeds deserve. But this man has done nothing wrong."

Then he said, "Jesus, remember me when you come into your kingdom."

Jesus answered him, "Truly I tell you, today you will be with me in paradise."

–Luke 23:39-43

In chapter 8 of *The Right Fight: How to Live a Loving Life*, the author discusses an illustration of the simplicity of Christianity found in the Gospel of Luke, where a convicted criminal is saved through nothing more than coming to know who and what Jesus is.

Jesus offers us salvation freely because of His love for us. Christianity is accepting that salvation and following His teachings, not because of the gifts He offers but out of gratitude for His goodness and our love for Him.

4. Although Christianity is not meant to be a religion, sometimes it becomes one. In what ways can we keep our focus when we find ourselves inclined to bargain with God?

_____

_____

_____

_____

_____

Just as the salvation we are given through the blood of Jesus Christ is the free gift of God, our following Him is also meant to be a gift, free of any expectations or demands on God. We are to walk in faith and follow in the ways of God because we love Him and not for anything He may or may not do for us in the future. Sometimes doing this is the hardest thing of all.

In the Book of Daniel, the Bible tells of three young men—Hananiah, Mishael, and Azariah—who were captured from Judah and brought to Babylon against their will. The three of them had occasion to express their love and devotion to God without any expectations or prerequisites, even under threat of death. You may have heard of them by the names they were given in Babylon: Shadrach, Meshach, and Abednego.

King Nebuchadnezzar made an image of gold, sixty cubits high and six cubits wide, and set it up on the plain of Dura in the province of Babylon. He then summoned the satraps, prefects, governors, advisers, treasurers, judges, magistrates and all the other provincial officials to come to the dedication of the image he had set up. So the satraps, prefects, governors, advisers, treasurers, judges, magistrates and all the other provincial officials assembled for the dedication of the image that King Nebuchadnezzar had set up, and they stood before it.

Then the herald loudly proclaimed, "Nations and peoples of every language, this is what you are commanded to do: As soon as you hear the sound of the horn, flute, zither, lyre, harp, pipe and all kinds of music, you must fall down and worship the image of gold that King Nebuchadnezzar has set up. Whoever does not fall down and worship will immediately be thrown into a blazing furnace."

Therefore, as soon as they heard the sound of the horn, flute, zither, lyre, harp and all kinds of music, all the nations and peoples of every language fell down and worshiped the image of gold that King Nebuchadnezzar had set up.

At this time some astrologers came forward and denounced the Jews. They said to King Nebuchadnezzar, "May the king live forever! Your Majesty has issued a decree that everyone who hears the sound of the horn, flute, zither, lyre, harp, pipe and all kinds of music must fall down and worship the image of gold, and that whoever does not fall down and worship will be thrown into a blazing furnace. But there are some Jews whom you have set over the affairs of the province of Babylon—Shadrach, Meshach and Abednego—who pay no attention to you, Your Majesty. They neither serve your gods nor worship the image of gold you have set up."

Furious with rage, Nebuchadnezzar summoned Shadrach, Meshach and Abednego. So these men were brought before the king, and Nebuchadnezzar said to them, "Is it true, Shadrach, Meshach and Abednego, that you do not serve my gods or worship the image of gold I have set up? Now when you hear the sound of the horn, flute, zither, lyre, harp, pipe and all kinds of music, if you are ready to fall down and worship the image I made, very good. But if you do not worship it, you will be thrown immediately into a blazing furnace. Then what god will be able to rescue you from my hand?"

Shadrach, Meshach and Abednego replied to him, "King Nebuchadnezzar, we do not need to defend ourselves before you in this matter. If we are thrown into the blazing furnace, the God we serve is able to deliver us from it, and he will deliver us from Your Majesty's hand. But even if he does not, we want you to know, Your Majesty, that we will not serve your gods or worship the image of gold you have set up."

Then Nebuchadnezzar was furious with Shadrach, Meshach and Abednego, and his attitude toward them changed. He ordered the furnace heated seven times hotter than usual and commanded some of the strongest soldiers in his army to tie up Shadrach, Meshach and Abednego and throw them into the blazing furnace. So these men, wearing their robes, trousers, turbans and other clothes, were bound and thrown into the blazing furnace. The king's command was so urgent and the furnace so hot that the flames of the fire killed the soldiers who took up Shadrach, Meshach and Abednego, and these three men, firmly tied, fell into the blazing furnace.

Then King Nebuchadnezzar leaped to his feet in amazement and asked his advisers, "Weren't there three men that we tied up and threw into the fire?"

They replied, "Certainly, Your Majesty."

He said, "Look! I see four men walking around in the fire, unbound and unharmed, and the fourth looks like a son of the gods."

Nebuchadnezzar then approached the opening of the blazing furnace and shouted, "Shadrach, Meshach and Abednego, servants of the Most High God, come out! Come here!"

So Shadrach, Meshach and Abednego came out of the fire, and the satraps, prefects, governors and royal advisers crowded around them. They saw that the fire had not harmed their bodies, nor was a hair of their heads singed; their robes were not scorched, and there was no smell of fire on them.

Then Nebuchadnezzar said, "Praise be to the God of Shadrach, Meshach and Abednego, who has sent his angel and rescued his servants! They trusted in him and defied the king's command and were willing to give up their lives rather than serve or worship any god except their own God. Therefore I decree that the people of any nation or language who say anything against the God of Shadrach, Meshach and Abednego be cut into pieces and their houses be turned into piles of rubble, for no other god can save in this way."

Then the king promoted Shadrach, Meshach and Abednego in the province of Babylon.

–Daniel 3

5. Shadrach, Meshach, and Abednego chose to honor and worship God alone, even when they were uncertain he would choose to save them from Nebuchadnezzar. Why is it important to trust and honor God even when we are not certain He will provide what we think we need?

_____

_____

_____

_____

_____

THE LOVE OF CHRIST

When we commit to a relationship with the one true God, the "source and foundation of all love," for His own sake and not for what He can do for us, the power of God's love really begins to work in our lives, no matter what our circumstances may be. We are enabled to live lives of love through our love for Jesus Christ, and we are able to love Him because of the love He has shown for us.

6. What happens when we root ourselves in the love of Christ? How does this nourish us in our journeys to live loving lives?

_____

_____

_____

_____

_____

7. Secular teaching tries to tell us that we are unable to love others unless we first love ourselves. Why will this approach always fail?

_____

_____

_____

_____

_____

> You see, at just the right time, when we were still
> powerless, Christ died for the ungodly. Very rarely
> will anyone die for a righteous person, though for
> a good person someone might possibly dare to die.
> But God demonstrates his own love for us in this:
> While we were still sinners, Christ died for us.
>
> —Romans 5:6–8

8. How does God's unconditional love for you lead you to respond to Him?

_____

_____

_____

_____

_____

9. How does it lead you to respond to others?

_____

_____

_____

_____

When we encounter the love of Christ, we can choose to respond to the sacrifice he made for us with gratitude and love in kind, or we can choose to refuse his gift. Like Judas, we can decide to value the approval of those in power, worldly possessions, temporary security, or comfort over the eternal redemption Christ offers us. This is a choice each person must make individually; Christianity is a one-on-one relationship. But it is important to remember that, like Judas, when we betray Christ Jesus, we are really betraying ourselves. For thirty pieces of silver, Judas sold away his place as one of Jesus's closest friends. We can do the same—or we can invest in our relationship with Jesus and grow in love for God and for others, as he means us to.

10. How can the choices we make in response to the message of Christ add or take away value to who we are as people?

_____

_____

_____

_____

_____

11. What choices take away value?

_____

_____

_____

_____

_____

12. What choices add value?

_____

_____

_____

_____

_____

Choosing a relationship with God—out of love for what He has already done for us and not out of any religiously motivated bargaining—is the best and truest way to grow in love for everyone. When we become rooted in God, His love begins to flow through us. His strength empowers us to look at others through the eyes of compassion, to try and try again to love when, in our fallen state, we keep failing. His love flows through us and out to transform every other relationship in our lives.

> I can do all things through Christ who strengthens me.
>
> –Philippians 4:13 (NKJV)

If you do not have this relationship with God, I urge you to ask the questions. Seek Him out! In Matthew 7:7, Jesus says, "Ask and it will be given to you; seek and you shall find; knock and the door will be opened to you." Our God does not leave people thirsty for Him wanting. His Son, Jesus Christ, has already died to atone for your sins and restore you to an eternity of abundant love—in this life and after death. All that's left for you to do is believe.

If you have already committed to a relationship with God, remember to feed into it! Abide in Christ, and He is more than happy to abide in you. Treat your relationship with Him like you would any other relationship that is important to you and better! Spend time with Jesus. Talk with Him. Introduce Him to your other friends. And as you do this, you will grow more like Him, His love will flow through you, and you will bear much fruit.

> When the disciples heard this, they were greatly astonished and asked, "Who then can be saved?" Jesus looked at them and said, "With man this is impossible, but with God all things are possible."
>
> –Matthew 19:25–26

APPLICATION

13. Do you have a personal relationship with God?

_____

_____

_____

_____

_____

14. If you have a relationship with God, have you been neglecting it lately? How can you prioritize your relationship with God this week?

_____

_____

_____

_____

_____

LESSON NINE

I Do, I Don't in Marriage

REVIEW

Last lesson, we studied how a relationship built on love with Christ—not a religion based on principles of bargaining—is the foundation for a fruitful life of love. Take some time to remember the importance of God's love in our lives.

1. How is Christianity different than other world religions?

_____

_____

_____

_____

_____

2. Why do Christians choose to love Christ?

_____

_____

_____

_____

_____

3. What effects does loving Christ have in the life of the Christian?

_____

_____

_____

_____

_____

THE RIGHT FIGHT IN MARRIAGE

In chapter 9 of *The Right Fight: How to Live a Loving Life,* the author switches gears. For the remainder of this study guide, as in the original book, we will be taking a look at the different areas love plays out in our lives.

One of the most immediate ways we see love play out—or fail—in everyday life is in marriage. There are countless ways in which we are called upon to exercise patience, kindness, honesty, trust, hope, persistence, and protectiveness in our relationships with the people who are closest to us. Conversely, it is often easiest to give into fearful and selfish emotions in marriage.

At the start of chapter 9 of *The Right Fight,* the author tells a story of how in the first year of his marriage, he and his wife, Tammie, fell into a disagreement because, while she wanted him to hold her at night, she wanted more for him to do this because he chose to, because he loved her, not just because she had asked. The author was faced with a situation where he could choose his own selfish comfort or choose to focus on his relationship with his wife.

In many, many situations, big and small, married couples must make decisions like this every day. We must all decide whether we choose love or a fearful, defensive selfishness. Fearful, defensive choices in marriage will cut off our roots. Loving choices will keep our marriages rooted in love and producing the fruit of blessings in our lives.

4. What is the difference between choices made for love and choices made out of obligation or with an underlying motive in a marriage?

_____

_____

_____

_____

_____

5. What are some positive outcomes of making choices that put your relationship with your spouse first?

_____

_____

_____

_____

_____

Being in Love versus Living in Love

We have studied how the misconceptions about love can be harmful to our relationships with others, and this is perhaps seen most obviously in marriage. Often, married couples feel their relationship is only working if they are "in love"—feeling the warm, affectionate feelings that follow as blessings when we are the seven things that love is to one another. But love is *not* a feeling, and when people married to one another stop tending the roots of love and making loving choices, they will not always feel the warm and fuzzy feelings secular culture mistakes for love itself.

6. How can marriages suffer when people mistake love for a feeling?

_____

_____

_____

_____

_____

7. How can married couples nurture the love between them even when loving feelings are absent?

_____

_____

_____

_____

_____

8. The author discusses how, in marriage, whenever one partner offends the other, initially it is often unintentional. Name some ways married couples can harm one another unintentionally.

_____

_____

_____

_____

_____

9. How can you keep the lines of communication open to let truth bless your marriage?

_____

_____

_____

_____

_____

Remember, love is not actually give and take. It is not about making a bargain, so it is never your responsibility to make sure someone else loves you. It is only your responsibility to love. Often, in marriage, partners blame one another for "making" them fall out of love, with the reasoning that if the other were more lovable, they would never have acted in an unloving way. This is toxic thinking! Each person is responsible for his or her own choices, and the bad behavior of one partner—from mild offenses like irritability at the end of the day to serious ones like infidelity—should never be blamed on the bad behavior of the other.

Take some time to list out what is your responsibility and what is not in a marriage.

My Responsibility (Loving My Spouse)	Not My Responsibility (My Spouse's Love for Me)

Love in Marriage: Case Study #1

Blake and Taylor have been married a year, and Taylor's frustration with Blake is building. During their courtship and engagement, the two of them had agreed that they would share household tasks once they were married. For the most part, this agreement has held up. Both Blake and Taylor take turns cooking meals and washing up during the week, and Blake alternates with Taylor doing other tasks as well—such as vacuuming, dusting, and putting things away—even though Blake's family is generally more relaxed about cleanliness than Taylor's. If Taylor does the laundry more often than Blake does, Taylor doesn't mind. But there is one task that Blake does not share with Taylor: Blake never takes out the garbage unless specifically asked to do so.

Without a garbage disposal in the kitchen sink of their older-model residence, the trash can develop an odor and attract insects if it is not regularly emptied, and Taylor hates this chore. It would be easier if Blake shared it with Taylor as with everything else, but even when Taylor leaves the trash for days until the trash lid does not close, Blake does not seem to get the hint to take a turn. Taylor feels silly, but Blake's neglect of this chore is becoming a source of resentment in their marriage. Nevertheless, Taylor can decide how to respond to Blake.

1. What fears might Taylor have in this situation? (What may be keeping Taylor from being open with Blake about the problem?)

2. How could truth make a path for a return to love and understanding for Taylor and Blake in this situation?

3. If Taylor is open with Blake and Blake does not change their behavior, how should Taylor respond in love?

LOVE MEANS ALWAYS SAYING YOU'RE SORRY

It is a popular saying that love means never saying you're sorry. People who say this generally mean that love always forgives, and this is true, but if God instructs us to ask Him when we need forgiveness—as he does in the Lord's Prayer in Matthew 6:9–13—we should be willing to ask one another when we need forgiveness as well. Healing after an offense in a relationship can only begin when we approach one another in a spirit of humility to mend the breach, and this is particularly important in marriage.

10. Why is it important to apologize when there is offense on either side of a relationship?

_____

_____

_____

_____

_____

> "Why do you look at the speck of sawdust in your brother's eye and pay no attention to the plank in your own eye? How can you say to your brother, 'Let me take the speck out of your eye,' when all the time there is a plank in your own eye? You hypocrite, first take the plank out of your own eye, and then you will see clearly to remove the speck from your brother's eye."
>
> –Matthew 7:3–5

11. When there is disagreement in a relationship, it can be tempting to allow pride to get the best of us and decide we will only reconcile after the other person apologizes for any fault, but this decision is rooted in the fearful perception that the person who apologizes first "loses" the argument and somehow appears weaker. How does apologizing for your own part in any disagreement put you on better footing than blaming your spouse?

_____

_____

_____

_____

_____

12. Why is forgiveness—both asking for it and giving it to others—so important in our journey to live lives of love?

_____

_____

_____

_____

_____

Love in Marriage: Case Study #2

Jamey and Parker's son, Cody, has been getting poor grades on his recent report cards. Jamey and Parker agree that they want their son to excel in school, developing habits of diligence that mean he can succeed even if the material at first seems difficult to him, so that he can have a good start in life. However, the two of them have found themselves in disagreement over the root causes of Cody's recent troubles and thus how they, as his parents, should respond to his bad grades.

Jamey has noticed that Cody seems more invested in extracurricular activities, such as basketball, art, and his relationships with his friends, than in his school work. Jamey believes that Cody may be prioritizing fun over his responsibilities to his education, and that as his parents, Jamey and Parker should stress the importance of meeting obligations before taking part in leisure activities and perhaps ground Cody from some of his extracurricular activities if his grades continue to be poor.

Parker has noticed that there has been a bigger drop in Cody's reading and social studies grades than in his math and science ones and that it is the word problems in math that he seems to struggle most with. Parker believes that Cody may be having difficulties with reading comprehension and that as his parents, Jamey and Parker should see if Cody perhaps could benefit from outside help in this area.

Jamey is reluctant to pay for Cody to receive additional tutoring in reading if he could improve his grades through additional attention to his studies, and Parker is reluctant to punish Cody if his grades are dropping due to a deeper learning difficulty instead of a lack of commitment. Cody himself has not been open about why his grades are dropping, and Jamey and Parker have begun to argue. Jamey has accused Parker of neglecting what could be a character problem in their son. Parker has accused Jamey of not believing in Cody and of caring more about money than about any trouble Cody may be having. Jamey and Parker are both hurt and angry now, and they have still not come to a solution on what to do about Cody's falling grades.

1. What fears might Jamey have in this situation? What fears might Parker have?

2. Love requires us to seek the truth in every situation. What are some of the ways Jamey and Parker could seek the truth of what is causing Cody's poor grades?

3. Regardless of how Jamey and Parker choose to respond to Cody's grades, how does love say they should resolve the disagreement between them and restore the peace in their marriage?

No marriage is perfect, just as no person is perfect. In the journey to live a loving life, in marriage—as in every other relationship in our lives—we will mess up again and again. Remember that it is our willingness to humble ourselves, apologize, and try again to seek the truth together that makes the difference between a life that is mostly ruled by love and a life that is mostly ruled by fear.

APPLICATION

13. What choices can you make to put your relationship with your spouse above your own feelings this week?

_____

_____

_____

_____

_____

14. Have you and your spouse fallen into disagreement over something lately, big or small, spoken or unspoken? What steps can you take to pursue understanding and mend your relationship? Remember—love demands that reconciliation begin with you.

_____

_____

_____

_____

_____

15. If you are not married, how can you apply the principles of selflessness and forgiveness in your own life this week?

_____

_____

_____

_____

NOTES

1. Huda, "Introduction and Resource Guide to Islam," Learn Religions, https://www.learnreligions.com/introduction-to-islam-2004096.

2. Library of Congress, "Hindu Rites and Rituals," Learn Religions, https://www.learnreligions.com/hindu-rites-and-rituals-1770058.

3. Subhamoy Das, "Find out How Hinduism Defines Dharma," Learn Religions, https://www.learnreligions.com/what-is-dharma-1770048.

4. Barbara O'Brien, "What Are the Four Noble Truths of Buddhism?," Learn Religions, https://www.learnreligions.com/the-four-noble-truths-450095.

5. Barbara O'Brien, "The Eightfold Path: The Way to Enlightenment in Buddhism," Learn Religions, https://www.learnreligions.com/the-eightfold-path-450067.

6. Ariela Pelaia, "Man or Messiah: The Role of Jesus in Judaism," Learn Religions, https://www.learnreligions.com/jewish-view-of-jesus-2076763.

7. Ariela Pelaia, "The Concept of Sin in Judaism," Learn Religions, https://www.learnreligions.com/do-jews-believe-in-sin-2076758.

Loving as a Leader

REVIEW

Love plays into every relationship and every aspect of our lives. In this lesson, we will study more about how we are to love in business situations, but do not forget that love is most easily seen and practiced every day at home.

1. What are some ways people most often let fear rule in their marriages?

    _____

    _____

    _____

    _____

    _____

2. Why is it important that each of us be willing to be the first to ask forgiveness when we fall into disagreement?

    _____

    _____

    _____

    _____

    _____

WHERE DO YOU LEAD?

If everyone in your entire place of business reports to you but that place of business is built upon their fear of you, you are not a leader—you are merely a boss. However, you do not have to be in charge of anyone or anything in your workplace to be a leader among your coworkers. Contrary to the beliefs of most people, leadership does not have to mean being in charge of others, but it always means inspiring others to follow with an attitude of loving service.

3. In your workplace and your interactions with others, are you more of a leader or a boss? How?

    _____

    _____

    _____

    _____

    _____

4. In *The Right Fight* chapter 10, the author mentions that true leaders love while they lead by sacrificing of themselves for others. What kind of sacrifices do we make at work for others? In other leadership positions in our lives?

    _____

    _____

    _____

    _____

    _____

LEADING BY PUTTING OTHERS FIRST

Just as we do in our relationships, in our work and businesses, we love by sacrificing ourselves and putting the needs of others first. When we choose to live out the seven things love is in our work, God's power flows through it and produces blessings in our places of business—healthy relationships with customers, clients, or partner businesses and trust in and outside the business.

5. The author gives one example of how putting others first in work and in business can bear fruit even if others take advantage of you. Name other ways conducting your work life ethically and with love, regardless of the actions of others, can bear fruit.

_____

_____

_____

_____

_____

6. Likewise, the author describes the way some businesses protect the short-term bottom line at the expense of the long-term fruitfulness of a business conducted with love. What are some other ways we, as leaders in the workplace and elsewhere, forget long-term fruitfulness in an effort to protect short-term blessings?

_____

_____

_____

_____

_____

APPLICATION

7. What are some ways you can set an example with your service to others in your workplace this week?

_____

_____

_____

_____

_____

8. How can you love your customers, clients, or business partners in what you do this week?

_____

_____

_____

_____

_____

Winning and Sports

REVIEW

Last lesson, we studied how love can be seen and bear fruit in the business world. Before we move on to discussing how love plays out in sports and leisure activities, take some more time to think about how we love others in the workplace and in our areas of leadership.

1. What are some differences between a leader and a boss? How does a person's relationship with love and fear play into this?

_____

_____

_____

_____

_____

2. What are some consequences businesses can suffer when leadership and employees allow fear and the defense of short-term profit to guide their actions rather than love for others?

_____

_____

THE COMPETITIVE PRINCIPLE

Sports and business are one and the same for many professional athletes and coaches across the world, but for most, participation in sports and games is an entirely different arena where we can choose to be controlled by fear or live out lives of love. There is something special about the competitive spirit in sports and games that heightens emotional responses. It can be all too easy to believe that winning is the only thing that matters. Fear can paralyze people on the field, court, or wherever they play and try to win, or it can drive them to pursue victory at any cost, sacrificing teammates and ethics in the process.

3. Has fear ever made you seize up in a sport or game? In another competitive setting?

----

4. Why are so many athletes and others driven by the fear of losing?

> For it is by grace you have been saved, through faith—and this is not from yourselves, it is the gift of God—not by works, so that no one can boast.
>
> –Ephesians 2:8–9

Many people in all areas of life, not just in athletics, believe that *winning* is what makes them valuable. The person who makes the most money, does the most work, or makes the best contribution is the most important. From very early childhood, we are conditioned to believe that our value is conditional upon our success.

However, in the light of Christ's love, our value is not dependent upon our performance in sports, at work, or anywhere in our lives. The fear of losing is powerful, and it is rooted in the perception that *losers are worth less than winners*. In sports and in life, it is important we remember that *nothing we do or win determines our value*. Instead, we are saved by God's grace and live our lives under the law of His love. Our value is determined by God, who created each of us unique and decided each of us was worth dying for.

THE REAL REASON TO WIN

If we don't want to win, why play sports at all? As the author observes in chapter 11 of *The Right Fight*, every athlete wants to win. But when our value is no longer dependent upon winning, the focus changes. If athletes keep rooted in the fundamentals—a love for the sport, for their teams, for the people watching, and for God—they soon find that they can give more than they ever did for a simple win. Their performance becomes a sacrifice, a selfless love offering to others.

5. How does offering your best to God and to the people watching your sport or labor change the focus?

_____

_____

_____

_____

_____

6. How can you focus on the fundamentals in your sport or hobby? What does this have to do with love?

_____

_____

_____

_____

_____

7. What is the difference between a team motivated by fear and a team motivated by love? How do these two different strategies play out long term in the sporting world and in life?

_____

_____

_____

_____

_____

In the story of Goliath, we see a boy who fights a battle, not for personal victory but for the love of God. David could not bear to hear God insulted by Goliath. He didn't fight Goliath for his own glory—he was aware that the battle was the Lord's. David fought Goliath to honor God, and his love for God gave him the strength to kill the giant.

In sports and in life, when we fight for God and others and stay rooted in the fundamentals of love, we become capable of more than we could have ever believed possible—not for our own glory but for His.

Now the Philistines gathered their forces for war and assembled at Sokoh in Judah. They pitched camp at Ephes Dammim, between Sokohand Azekah. Saul and the Israelites assembled and camped in the Valley of Elah and drew up their battle line to meet the Philistines. The Philistines occupied one hill and the Israelites another, with the valley between them.

A champion named Goliath, who was from Gath, came out of the Philistine camp. His height was six cubits and a span. He had a bronze helmet on his head and wore a coat of scale armor of bronze weighing five thousand shekels; on his legs he wore bronze greaves, and a bronze javelin was slung on his back. His spear shaft was like a weaver's rod, and its iron point weighed six hundred shekels. His shield bearer went ahead of him.

Goliath stood and shouted to the ranks of Israel, "Why do you come out and line up for battle? Am I not a Philistine, and are you not the servants of Saul? Choose a man and have him come down to me. If he is able to fight and kill me, we will become your subjects; but if I overcome him and kill him, you will become our subjects and serve us." Then the Philistine said, "This day I defy the armies of Israel! Give me a man and let us fight each other." On hearing the Philistine's words, Saul and all the Israelites were dismayed and terrified.

Now David was the son of an Ephrathite named Jesse, who was from Bethlehem in Judah. Jesse had eight sons, and in Saul's time he was very old. Jesse's three oldest sons had followed Saul to the war: The firstborn was Eliab; the second, Abinadab; and the third, Shammah. David was the youngest. The three oldest followed Saul, but David went back and forth from Saul to tend his father's sheep at Bethlehem.

For forty days the Philistine came forward every morning and evening and took his stand.

Now Jesse said to his son David, "Take this ephah of roasted grain and these ten loaves of bread for your brothers and hurry to their camp. Take along these ten cheeses to the commander of their unit. See how your brothers are and bring back some assurance from them. They are with Saul and all the men of Israel in the Valley of Elah, fighting against the Philistines."

Early in the morning David left the flock in the care of a shepherd, loaded up and set out, as Jesse had directed. He reached the camp as the army was going out to its battle positions, shouting the war cry. Israel and the Philistines were drawing up their lines facing each other.

David left his things with the keeper of supplies, ran to the battle lines and asked his brothers how they were. As he was talking with them, Goliath, the Philistine champion from Gath, stepped out from his lines and shouted his usual defiance, and David heard it. Whenever the Israelites saw the man, they all fled from him in great fear.

Now the Israelites had been saying, "Do you see how this man keeps coming out? He comes out to defy Israel. The king will give great wealth to the man who kills him. He will also give him his daughter in marriage and will exempt his family from taxes in Israel."

David asked the men standing near him, "What will be done for the man who kills this Philistine and removes this disgrace from Israel? Who is this uncircumcised Philistine that he should defy the armies of the living God?"

They repeated to him what they had been saying and told him, "This is what will be done for the man who kills him."

When Eliab, David's oldest brother, heard him speaking with the men, he burned with anger at him and asked, "Why have you come down here? And with whom did you leave those few sheep in the wilderness? I know how conceited you are and how wicked your heart is; you came down only to watch the battle."

"Now what have I done?" said David. "Can't I even speak?" He then turned away to someone else and brought up the same matter, and the men answered him as before. What David said was overheard and reported to Saul, and Saul sent for him.

David said to Saul, "Let no one lose heart on account of this Philistine; your servant will go and fight him."

Saul replied, "You are not able to go out against this Philistine and fight him; you are only a young man, and he has been a warrior from his youth."

But David said to Saul, "Your servant has been keeping his father's sheep. When a lion or a bear came and carried off a sheep from the flock, I went after it, struck it and rescued the sheep from its mouth. When it turned on me, I seized it by its hair, struck it and killed it. Your servant has killed both the lion and the bear; this uncircumcised Philistine will be like one of them, because he has defied the armies of the living God. The Lord who rescued me from the paw of the lion and the paw of the bear will rescue me from the hand of this Philistine."

Saul said to David, "Go, and the Lord be with you."

Then Saul dressed David in his own tunic. He put a coat of armor on him and a bronze helmet on his head. David fastened on his sword over the tunic and tried walking around, because he was not used to them.

"I cannot go in these," he said to Saul, "because I am not used to them." So he took them off. Then he took his staff in his hand, chose five smooth stones from the stream, put them in the pouch of his shepherd's bag and, with his sling in his hand, approached the Philistine.

Meanwhile, the Philistine, with his shield bearer in front of him, kept coming closer to David. He looked David over and saw that he was little more than a boy, glowing with health and handsome, and he despised him. He said to David, "Am I a dog, that you come at me with sticks?" And the Philistine cursed David by his gods. "Come here," he said, "and I'll give your flesh to the birds and the wild animals!"

David said to the Philistine, "You come against me with sword and spear and javelin, but I come against you in the name of the Lord Almighty, the God of the armies of Israel, whom you have defied. This day the Lord will deliver you into my hands, and I'll strike you down and cut off your head. This very day I will give the carcasses of the Philistine army to the birds and the wild animals, and the whole world will know that there is a God in Israel. All those gathered here will know that it is not by sword or spear that the Lord saves; for the battle is the Lord's, and he will give all of you into our hands."

As the Philistine moved closer to attack him, David ran quickly toward the battle line to meet him. Reaching into his bag and taking out a stone, he slung it and struck the Philistine on the forehead. The stone sank into his forehead, and he fell facedown on the ground.

So David triumphed over the Philistine with a sling and a stone; without a sword in his hand he struck down the Philistine and killed him.

David ran and stood over him. He took hold of the Philistine's sword and drew it from the sheath. After he killed him, he cut off his head with the sword.

When the Philistines saw that their hero was dead, they turned and ran. Then the men of Israel and Judah surged forward with a shout and pursued the Philistines to the entrance of Gath and to the gates of Ekron. Their dead were strewn along the Shaaraim road to Gath and Ekron. When the Israelites returned from chasing the Philistines, they plundered their camp.

David took the Philistine's head and brought it to Jerusalem; he put the Philistine's weapons in his own tent.

As Saul watched David going out to meet the Philistine, he said to Abner, commander of the army, "Abner, whose son is that young man?"

Abner replied, "As surely as you live, Your Majesty, I don't know."

The king said, "Find out whose son this young man is."

As soon as David returned from killing the Philistine, Abner took him and brought him before Saul, with David still holding the Philistine's head.

"Whose son are you, young man?" Saul asked him.

David said, "I am the son of your servant Jesse of Bethlehem."

–1 Samuel 17

APPLICATION

8. How can you keep the focus on love in your sport?

_____

_____

_____

_____

_____

9. Why is it important not to think about love helping you win?

_____

_____

_____

_____

_____

10. Who or what do you play and fight for?

_____

_____

_____

_____

_____

LESSON TWELVE

Loving in Your Influence

REVIEW

Last lesson, we studied how focusing on the fundamentals of love can help us overcome the fear of failure when we compete, in sports and in life. Take some time to review how we can dedicate our performance—athletic or otherwise—to God, to the sport, to our team, and to the people important to us and so stay rooted in love.

1. Explain the fear of losing that haunts many people in and outside of athletics. What is the root of this fear?

   _____

   _____

   _____

   _____

   _____

2. How do we fight the fear of failure in sports and elsewhere in our lives?

   _____

   _____

   _____

_____

_____

3. How does dedicating our performance to the glory of God and others give us strength?

_____

_____

_____

_____

_____

Spheres of Influence

When we live our lives in love, the impact will ripple out and affect the lives of others. Conversely, if we choose to live in fear, the people around us will see that and take notice. We are all living at the center of a sphere of influence that reaches our families, our friends, and our communities. Some individuals, such as former President George H. W. Bush in the author's anecdote in chapter 12, have larger spheres of influence than others, but everyone has an effect upon someone.

4. How is influence over someone different from leadership over them? Give an example.

_____

_____

_____

_____

_____

5. Who in your life do you have influence over? This can be employees, acquaintances, friends, or family.

_____

_____

_____

_____

_____

THE IMPACT OF LOVE

Our loving or fearful actions are both seen and felt by others. We can choose to live out our lives as a blessing or to selfishly ignore the impact our choices and attitudes have on other people. The proof, as always, will be in the fruit we bear.

6. What are the fruits of a loving home? A loving business? What do you notice first about a loving environment?

_____

_____

_____

_____

_____

7. Describe a time someone has acted with genuine love toward you.

_____

_____

_____

_____

_____

8. Do you find yourself setting expectations before you are kind and courteous toward others? Do you more often expect reciprocation or some favor for your courtesy, or do you find you can love others without expectation or resentment when your kindness is unappreciated or unreturned?

_____

_____

_____

_____

_____

A Powerful Way to Love

Whether you are famous, popular, an influence to many, or simply the most powerful influence in the lives of your children each day, the selfless love you invest into your relationships with others will be remembered. The example we set has perhaps its biggest impact on our children, but other family members, coworkers, employees, neighbors, and friends can all be touched and influenced through a life lived in love.

9. In a world where people seem busier every day, time can be the biggest investment you can make in others. What are some ways you can sacrifice your time for others?

_____

_____

_____

_____

_____

10. How does sacrificing your time strengthen your influence over others?

_____

_____

_____

_____

_____

11. How does the sacrifice of your time impact those over whom you already have an influence?

_____

_____

_____

_____

_____

APPLICATION

12. How can you be more mindful of the individuals in your life you have influence over this week?

_____

_____

_____

_____

13. Name some individuals in your sphere of influence who might need to see genuine love this week. How can you reach out to them?

_____

_____

_____

_____

_____

14. Who can you give your time to this week? In what ways?

_____

_____

_____

_____

_____

Little Blue House

REVIEW

We're coming to the last four lessons of our study in *The Right Fight*. Last lesson, we discussed how each of us influences the people around us with the actions we take and especially by giving or withholding our time.

1. How do your rudeness, impatience, and selfishness leave an impact on those you come into contact with? How can your loving acts of self-sacrifice leave an impression instead?

_____

_____

_____

_____

_____

2. Who are some people we have influence over? In what ways?

_____

_____

_____

_____

_____

SEEING THE FORGOTTEN

We've discussed how love impacts others when we are visible, but this week's lesson is about how love reaches out and touches the lives of those who feel *invisible*. Love can have the biggest effect on those who, like the little blue house in the author's anecdote in chapter 13 of *The Right Fight*, feel overlooked, ignored, and forgotten. Kindness and protectiveness toward people who are struggling with these feelings stretches farther than it does anywhere else. We know this because each of us remembers the people who have taken the time to love us when we felt this way.

3. Think of a time when you felt left out or forgotten. What helped you through that time?

_____

_____

_____

_____

_____

4. God shows his favor to the left out and forgotten—the little blue houses of this world. If we are His hands and feet on Earth, what is our responsibility toward the poor and neglected around us?

_____

_____

_____

_____

_____

"Blessed are the poor in spirit, for theirs is the kingdom of heaven.

Blessed are those who mourn, for they will be comforted.

Blessed are the meek, for they will inherit the earth.

Blessed are those who hunger and thirst for righteousness, for they will be filled.

Blessed are the merciful, for they will be shown mercy.

Blessed are the pure in heart, for they will see God."

"Blessed are the peacemakers, for they will be called children of God.

"Blessed are those who are persecuted because of righteousness, for theirs is the kingdom of heaven.

"Blessed are you when people insult you, persecute you and falsely say all kinds of evil against you because of me. Rejoice and be glad, because great is your reward in heaven, for in the same way they persecuted the prophets who were before you.

"You are the salt of the earth. But if the salt loses its saltiness, how can it be made salty again? It is no longer good for anything, except to be thrown out and trampled underfoot.

"You are the light of the world. A town built on a hill cannot be hidden. Neither do people light a lamp and put it under a bowl. Instead they put it on its stand, and it gives light to everyone in the house. In the same way, let your light shine before others, that they may see your good deeds and glorify your Father in heaven."

–Matthew 5:3–15

5. What are some ways we can make the overlooked in our lives feel valued?

_____

_____

_____

_____

_____

6. Remember, no one can measure up to God's standards of love and acceptance all the time. Why is it important to forgive ourselves when we fall short?

_____

_____

_____

_____

_____

7. While we must never put ourselves before others, there are many individuals who believe they, like the little blue house, are unworthy of notice at all—either nothing special in and of themselves or beyond compassion due to what they may have done. Where can we look for comfort when we feel unworthy?

_____

_____

_____

_____

_____

THE TRUE VALUE OF AN INDIVIDUAL

The author says in chapter 13 of *The Right Fight* that "every person has equal value regardless of their current circumstances. Performance and finances and social status don't determine anyone's worth."

Value traditionally has two measures: origins and substance and what someone is willing to pay. For example, a work of art by a master craftsman has a higher original value than a work by a student, but time and demand can make any work of art worth more—if people are willing to pay more for it.

Each of us was made unique, wonderful, and with the utmost care by the best craftsman there is: God Himself. When we became lost to sin, His son Jesus was willing to sacrifice everything to buy us back. Even when we are tempted to devalue others and overlook

> "Teacher, which is the greatest commandment in the Law?"
>
> Jesus replied: "'Love the Lord your God with all your heart and with all your soul and with all your mind.' This is the first and greatest commandment. And the second is like it: 'Love your neighbor as yourself.' All the Law and the Prophets hang on these two commandments."
>
> –Matthew 22:36–40

them like the little blue house because they are poor or disabled or look different or think in different ways, or even when we feel we ourselves are overlooked and unworthy, love remembers that God has placed the ultimate value on every one of us. Who are we to disagree?

8. How does it free you to know that your value is not based on what you do or own?

_____

_____

_____

_____

_____

APPLICATION

9. Do you need to receive forgiveness this week? How or why?

_____

_____

_____

_____

_____

10. Name some people in your life that might feel unworthy and overlooked.

_____

_____

_____

_____

11. How can you show these people love this week?

_____

_____

_____

_____

_____

When Love Means

Walking Away

REVIEW

Last lesson, we discussed how, as individuals rooted in God's love and dedicated to extending it to others, we must look beyond appearances and reach out to the overlooked and forgotten in our communities, aware that God loves and values every person on earth. When we ourselves feel overlooked and forgotten, we can take encouragement from the fact that God made each of us unique and special and gave His son Jesus to save us.

1. How does influence reach further when we reach out to the poor, overlooked, and forgotten in our communities? How much more do you remember the people who have reached out to you when you were feeling small?

_____

_____

_____

_____

_____

2. Where do we find our worth?

_____

_____

_____

_____

_____

WHAT ABOUT ABUSE?

Love teaches us that each of us finds our worth in God and in Jesus Christ, His son. He created us, and Jesus died to save us from our sins, so no one ever needs to be ashamed or unworthy. But, as we know, there are people in the world who go past overlooking others. They give in, allow their lives to be ruled by fear and anger and selfishness, and become abusive toward others.

Chapter 14 of *The Right Fight* discusses how loving individuals should respond to people who persist in abuse. There is an enormous difference between remaining open, trusting, and loving when another person inadvertently offends or betrays you or lashes out occasionally in fear versus allowing yourself to be repeatedly and willfully abused.

In situations that have become toxic and abusive, **there is no shame in leaving an abuser.** Not only is the cycle of abuse toxic for the person who is abused, but, as we have seen, abusers cut off their own roots from love and harm themselves when they choose to steal the blessings of others and act in anger, envy, or malice. In fact, it is better for both people involved in such a relationship if the person being abused walks away. It is a loving thing to refuse to allow an abuser to continue to live a fruitless life, and it is not selfish to refuse to live in a situation where you are experiencing abuse.

3. How is it unhealthy for an abuser if the person they are abusing enables this
    behavior by remaining?

_____

_____

_____

_____

_____

4.   What effects does abuse have on the abuser?

_____

_____

_____

_____

_____

5.   How can we tell when love demands we *do* protect ourselves?

_____

_____

_____

_____

_____

Abuse is just an extreme variety of other instances where individuals allow themselves to be ruled by fear. It manifests when abusers are afraid of losing control, when they are afraid of being abandoned, when they allow themselves to be so dominated by their feelings of hurt, pride, or anger that they decide to sacrifice others to those feelings. In effect, abusers become dependent in one or more ways upon the people they abuse. Fruitless themselves because they have cut off their roots from love, they must rely entirely upon the fruit of others to sustain themselves.

A loving person who has been abused, despite how it may seem, is not in so desperate of a situation.

When to Walk Away

Sometimes it can be difficult to tell when abuse is taking place, in your home or relationship or in someone else's. When you care about someone else, it can be difficult to leave, no matter what the situation, and many abused individuals may be inclined to make excuses for their abusers. Below are some examples of abuse that merits walking away:

- Repeated physical abuse or warnings of physical abuse—violently hitting or using the environment in an effort to intimidate.

- Sexual abuse, including molestation, degradation, and instances of marital rape.

- Conscious and manipulative emotional and verbal abuse intended to belittle or make the abused wholly dependent on the abuser and distrustful of their own ability or perceptions; gaslighting.

6. If a person who has been abused has to leave in order to protect themselves and stop enabling their abusers, if they are forced to find a new home or even a new community, what is left to them if they continue in love?

_____

_____

_____

_____

_____

If You Are Being Abused or Know Someone Who Is

If you are being abused or know someone who is, get help. Get out. There are some resources listed below to help you report abuse taking place and, if you are the person being abused, to leave your situation safely and find professional help.

The resources below skew toward women. Statistically, women are at a higher risk for physical or sexual abuse than men are, but they are also more likely to report their situation. Many men and boys also experience abuse, and studies suspect the number is far higher than is reported. No one should be ashamed or afraid to seek help if they are being abused, and many resources that market themselves toward women are also more than willing to help men experiencing abuse.

To Report Abuse

- National Child Abuse Hotline: 1-800-422-4453
- National Domestic Violence Hotline: 1-800-799-7233
- National Sexual Assault Hotline:1-800-656-4673
- Resources on Recognizing the Sources of Abuse
- Mayo Clinic: MayoClinic.org/healthy-lifestyle/adult-health/in -depth/domestic-violence/art-20048397
- Harvard Women's Health Watch: Health.Harvard.edu/newsletter _article/recognizing-domestic-partner-abuse

Finding a Place to Go

- Women'sShelters.org—emergency shelters, domestic violence shelters, family shelters, and transitional shelters: WomenShelters.org/
- DomesticShelters.org—further information, resources, and access to aid programs and emergency shelters: DomesticShelters.org/
- Women'sLaw.org—further resources, legal information, and emergency shelters: WomensLaw.org/

Unexpected Blessings of Love

LOVE CAN TAKE YOU BY SURPRISE

From the beginning of this study, we have emphasized getting into the *right fight*—living a loving life not for the sake of the fruit or blessings that result from it but out of a true devotion to God

> "But many who are first will be last, and many who are last will be first."
>
> –Matthew 19:30

and to the well-being of others. The paradox of doing this is that while the blessings of living a loving life may not come immediately and may not look like what most would expect, they are the truest and sweetest blessings there are, and all the more so because they come as surprises.

1. Was there ever a time where you acted in love or humility, expecting no reward, and reaped an unexpected blessing? Share your own story.

_____

_____

_____

_____

_____

What Is the State of Your Garden?

It's important that we remember to stay in the *right fight*: that we choose to act in love for the good of others and to maintain a relationship with God, and not because of the blessings we receive as a result. At the same time, it is true that the fruit we see in our lives—the richness of our relationships with others, the closeness of our families and communities, and the trust others have in us, among other things—can serve as an indicator of the state of our roots. Likewise, if our relationships are strained and full of distrust and hurtful words, if our homes and families become cold and distant, it can reveal that we may have been making selfish choices motivated instead by our feelings of fear.

2. What do you notice about the world around you? Is it filled with the rewards of loving, well-connected roots, or is your tree barren and disconnected?

    _____

    _____

    _____

    _____

> "By their fruit you will recognize them. Do people pick grapes from thornbushes, or figs from thistles? Likewise, every good tree bears good fruit, but a bad tree bears bad fruit. A good tree cannot bear bad fruit, and a bad tree cannot bear good fruit. Every tree that does not bear good fruit is cut down and thrown into the fire. Thus, by their fruit you will recognize them.
>
> —Matthew 7:16–20

3. Are you living out of love for God and for others or out of fear for yourself?

_____

_____

_____

_____

_____

4. How can the fruit of love renew your life?

_____

_____

_____

_____

_____

APPLICATION

5. How can you reach out to bless others this week?

_____

_____

_____

_____

_____

6. If you take inventory of the fruit your life is producing, what do you notice about the state of your roots?

_____

_____

_____

_____

_____

7. How can you love God more?

_____

_____

_____

_____

8. How can you love others more?

_____

_____

_____

_____

From the Heart

REVIEW

We've discussed how when we focus on the right fight and put others before ourselves, love can fill our lives with the truest, most unexpected blessings. While, paradoxically, focusing solely on these blessings can lead to our roots withering as we selfishly try to keep our fruit all for ourselves or get more and more, being aware of the fruitfulness or fruitlessness of our lives can give us important clues about the state of our roots.

1. What sort of blessings do the roots of love produce in our lives? How might they be different than others expect?

    _____

    _____

    _____

    _____

2. When others offend us or take advantage of us—living off the blessings that love has produced in our lives and taking our fruit—what should our response be?

    _____

    _____

_____

_____

_____

THE TAKEAWAY

If you take one thing away from this study, let it be this: what rules your heart rules your actions and decisions and, ultimately, determines whether love or fear rules your life. The roots of love—patience, kindness, truthfulness, protectiveness, trust, hope, and perseverance—die or stay healthy depending on how they are nourished in the soil that surrounds them. Independently, each of us is incapable of living a life that is loving all of the time: just as a tree pulled up by the roots dies, so do we. We have to draw our nourishment from somewhere.

3. How does what you think about and believe in determine how you live your life?

_____

_____

_____

_____

_____

For a group: Discuss ways people can fill
their minds and hearts with the love of God.
Suggestions include regular church attendance
or participation in a Bible study (involvement in
a godly community), a daily or semiweekly quiet
time (immersion in the Word of God), Scripture
memorization and meditation, and volunteering.

"I am the vine; you are the branches. If you remain in me and I in you, you will bear much fruit; apart from me you can do nothing. If you do not remain in me, you are like a branch that is thrown away and withers; such branches are picked up, thrown into the fire and burned. If you remain in me and my words remain in you, ask whatever you wish, and it will be done for you. This is to my Father's glory, that you bear much fruit, showing yourselves to be my disciples.

"As the Father has loved me, so have I loved you. Now remain in my love. If you keep my commands, you will remain in my love, just as I have kept my Father's commands and remain in his love."

–John 15:5–10

When we root in Christ, find our nourishment in Him, God's love flows through every part of us. His power sustains us. It enables us to move beyond the fearful emotions of a moment and see the truth. His love for others enables us to love others when on our own we couldn't do it. And as we live in His love, our lives begin to bear fruit, and we are blessed and go on to bless others.

4. How can you stay rooted in the love of God?

_____

_____

_____

_____

_____

5. From where do you draw your nourishment?

_____

_____

_____

_____

_____

6. What do words reveal about a person's thoughts and beliefs?

_____

_____

_____

_____

_____

7. What do your words reveal about your thoughts and beliefs?

_____

_____

_____

_____

_____

> "You brood of vipers, how can you who
> are evil say anything good? For the mouth
> speaks what the heart is full of."
>
> —Matthew 12:34

Throughout this study, we have discussed the difference between the popular conception of what love means and what it actually means. One of the most common clichés that we hear is that you cannot love others until you first love yourself. In chapter 16 of *The Right Fight*, the author discusses how this conventional wisdom twists the actual truth: that you actually cannot love others properly until love rules your life.

8. What is the difference between being unable to love others until you first love yourself and being unable to love others until love rules your life? Explain.

_____

_____

_____

_____

_____

THE HEALING OF A HEART

Life isn't easy. People make mistakes and accidentally hurt others. Sometimes they act out of malice and deliberately try to hurt others. At one time or another, we all end up with our fruit stolen and crushed, with our hearts broken, intentionally or otherwise or simply because temporary and permanent losses are parts of our existence this side of heaven. When our hearts are broken, it can be tempting to build that wall, to detach from others and protect ourselves from further hurt—but this is a fear-based reaction that, far from preserving us from further pain, can actually keep us from healing. Living in fear keeps us from growing past the pain and producing more fruit; only living out the seven things love is can heal a broken heart.

9. How does loving others heal the hurt of a broken heart?

_____

_____

_____

_____

_____

In the end, all that is truly needed to begin living out the seven things love is, healing a broken heart, and transforming a life with love is to love Jesus. Like the criminal on the cross next to Jesus, who transformed his destiny in a moment even as he died by seeing the truth of Jesus's innocence and humbly asking Jesus to remember him, each of us is transformed forever when we choose to love Jesus and submit to Him. In effect, we become entirely new people, and if we continue in the love of Christ, his love transforms us for the rest of our lives.

10. What changes do we see in our lives when we love God first and most?

_____

_____

_____

_____

_____

If you have not committed to love God first and most, He can come into your life. Romans 10:9–10 says, "If you declare with your mouth, 'Jesus is Lord,' and believe in your heart that God raised him from the dead, you will be saved. For it is with your heart that you believe and are justified, and it is with your mouth that you profess your faith and are saved." When you make the choice to believe in Jesus and put Him first, His power will work through you and help you live a life ruled by His love, here and into eternity.

If you have given your life to Christ already but have neglected your relationship with Him lately, withdrawing your roots from Him, don't worry. The choice to abide in Christ is one we can make again every day. Every day, we can recommit to loving God and putting Him first. Every day, we can decide to make choices ruled by that love.

Now there was a Pharisee, a man named Nicodemus who was a member of the Jewish ruling council. He came to Jesus at night and said, "Rabbi, we know that you are a teacher who has come from God. For no one could perform the signs you are doing if God were not with him."

Jesus replied, "Very truly I tell you, no one can see the kingdom of God unless they are born again."

"How can someone be born when they are old?" Nicodemus asked. "Surely they cannot enter a second time into their mother's womb to be born!"

Jesus answered, "Very truly I tell you, no one can enter the kingdom of God unless they are born of water and the Spirit. Flesh gives birth to flesh, but the Spirit gives birth to spirit. You should not be surprised at my saying, 'You must be born again.' The wind blows wherever it pleases. You hear its sound, but you cannot tell where it comes from or where it is going. So it is with everyone born of the Spirit."

"How can this be?" Nicodemus asked.

"You are Israel's teacher," said Jesus, "and do you not understand these things? Very truly I tell you, we speak of what we know, and we testify to what we have seen, but still you people do not accept our testimony. I have spoken to you of earthly things and you do not believe; how then will you believe if I speak of heavenly things? No one has ever gone into heaven except the one who came from heaven—the Son of Man. Just as Moses lifted up the snake in the wilderness, so the Son of Man must be lifted up, that everyone who believes may have eternal life in him.

"For God so loved the world that he gave his one and only Son, that whoever believes in him shall not perish but have eternal life. For God did not send his Son into the world to condemn the world, but to save the world through him. Whoever believes in him is not condemned, but whoever does not believe stands condemned already because they have not believed in the name of God's one and only Son. This is the verdict: Light has come into the world, but people loved darkness instead of light because their deeds were evil. Everyone who does evil hates the light, and will not come into the light for fear that their deeds will be exposed. But whoever lives by the truth comes into the light, so that it may be seen plainly that what they have done has been done in the sight of God.

–John 3:1–21

When our lives are ruled by the love of Christ, His love will overflow. We will bear so much fruit we will find we are unable to keep it all. The blessings of love will spill over into the lives of others. God gives them to us to give away. People who abide in God's love will have a natural desire to share that love with others—not only in the choices they make but in their words: they will want to tell others about the love they have found.

As you leave this study, I hope you leave it with a greater understanding of love, how it is the fundamental law for a life well lived and reaches out through everything. I hope you leave this study feeling closer to the God who is the source of all our love. And as you walk forth in His light, I hope you love.

Review

This space is for readers who have already gone through *The Right Fight Study Guide*. It allows for a recap of the book's major concepts but should not be considered a separate lesson. Groups making use of *The Right Fight Study Guide* may nevertheless wish to go over the review either at the opening or the conclusion of the final lesson to cap the study.

1. What does it mean to lovingly sacrifice yourself?

    _____

    _____

    _____

    _____

    _____

2. How is love the fundamental principle for living a good life?

    _____

    _____

    _____

    _____

3. Why is it important to view love or fear as choices we can make instead of feelings?

    _____

    _____

_____

_____

_____

4. How can seeking the hidden truths behind the actions of others help us to make loving decisions?

    _____

    _____

    _____

    _____

    _____

5. What traps can living based on our emotions lead us into?

    _____

    _____

    _____

    _____

    _____

6. Why is it important to focus on making loving choices instead of what we feel because of them?

    _____

    _____

    _____

    _____

    _____

7. What does the fruit of a loving life look like?

_____

_____

_____

_____

_____

8. In what way is Christianity different from other religions in its approach to love and salvation?

_____

_____

_____

_____

_____

9. What are some ways in which love is easiest seen in marriage? What are some ways love is hardest and most important to practice in marriage?

_____

_____

_____

_____

10. How are those who put others first leaders?

_____

_____

_____

_____

_____

11. Why do people in sports and other walks of life experience the fear of losing? How do we change the focus and let love rule in the competitive arenas of our lives?

_____

_____

_____

_____

_____

12. What is one of the most meaningful, loving ways we can sacrifice for others?

_____

_____

_____

_____

13. How does love measure the value of a person?

_____

_____

_____

_____

14. In what kinds of situations does love demand we do protect ourselves? Why is this the case?

_____

_____

_____

_____

_____

15. How can the fruit of love renew your life?

_____

_____

_____

_____

_____

16. How does what you think about and believe in determine how you live your life?

_____

_____

_____

_____

_____

About the Author

Kenny Vaughan is a husband, a father, a world-class athlete, and a servant of Jesus Christ. Over the years, he has been featured in a number of interviews with national media, and his Instagram video posts (@johnkennedyvaughan) about love and faith inspire tens of thousands across the country.

Growing up, Kenny learned to water ski, to hunt and fish, to understand God's perfect love, and to honor God, country, and family. For fifteen years, he chased his dream of winning the national water ski long-jump championship, and, bolstered by the scriptures scrawled on his ski tow-rope handles, he achieved his dream. Vaughan took the scriptures that inspired him that day and had them inscribed on dog tags. He founded Shields of Strength, a company that distributes inspirational scripture engraved upon dog tags and other jewelry. The necklaces have become popular with professional and aspiring athletes—including Olympians, military personnel, law enforcement, students, and adults from all walks of life who find encouragement in scripture to face life's challenges.

When Vaughan published his second book with Brown Books, *The Right Fight: How to Live a Loving Life*, he began to receive overwhelming responses from those whose lives were being changed through understanding the true meaning of love. Churches and small groups asked for a workbook to help them delve even more deeply into God's plan for choosing love over fear. *The Right Fight Study Guide* will, Kenny hopes, be a companion for readers of *The Right Fight* who wish to navigate a journey on how God's love works in their own lives.

Kenny is also the author of *Shields of Strength: One Man's Victory over Fear and What It Has Meant for America.*

Kenny Vaughan lives in Southeast Texas, near Beaumont, with Tammie, the love of his life, and their three children.